eary, D 8/20

Hold Slip

THE LAND I LOST
ADVENTURES OF A BOY IN VIETNAM

by Huynh Quang Nhuong
with pictures by Vo-Dinh Mai

HarperTrophy
A Division of HarperCollinsPublishers

The Land I Lost
Text copyright © 1982 by Huynh Quang Nhuong
Illustrations copyright © 1982 by Vo-Dinh Mai

Library of Congress Cataloging-in-Publication Data
Huynh, Quang Nhuong.
   The land I lost.
   Summary: A collection of personal reminiscences of
the author's youth in a hamlet on the central highlands
of Vietnam.
   1. Central Highlands (Vietnam)—Social life and
customs—Juvenile literature.   2. Huynh, Quang Nhuong—
Juvenile literature.   3. Central Highlands (Vietnam)—
Biography—Juvenile literature.   [1. Huynh, Quang Nhuong.
2. Central Highlands (Vietnam)—Biography]   I. Vo-Dinh
Mai, ill   II.   Title.
DS559.92.C46H88   1982   959.7 [92]   80-8437
ISBN 0-397-32447-2   AACR2
ISBN 0-397-32448-0 (lib. bdg.)
ISBN 0-06-440183-9 (pbk.)

First Harper Trophy Edition, 1986.

For my mother

CONTENTS

THE LAND I LOST

I was born on the central highlands of Vietnam in a small hamlet on a riverbank that had a deep jungle on one side and a chain of high mountains on the other. Across the river, rice fields stretched to the slopes of another chain of mountains.

There were fifty houses in our hamlet, scattered along the river or propped against the mountainsides. The houses were made of bamboo and covered with coconut leaves, and each was surrounded by a deep trench to protect it from wild animals or thieves. The only way to enter a house was to walk across a "monkey bridge"—a single bamboo stick that spanned the trench. At night we pulled the bridges into our houses and were safe.

There were no shops or marketplaces in our hamlet. If we needed supplies—medicine, cloth, soaps, or candles—we had to cross over the mountains and travel to a town nearby. We used the river mainly for traveling to distant hamlets, but it also provided us with plenty of fish.

During the six-month rainy season, nearly all of us helped plant and cultivate fields of rice, sweet potatoes, Indian mustard, eggplant, tomatoes, hot peppers, and corn. But during the dry season, we became hunters and turned to the jungle.

Wild animals played a very large part in our lives. There were four animals we feared the most: the tiger, the lone wild hog, the crocodile, and the horse snake. Tigers were always trying to steal cattle. Sometimes, however, when a tiger became old and slow it became a maneater. But a lone wild hog was even more dangerous than a tiger. It attacked every creature in sight, even when it had no need for food. Or it did crazy things, such as charging into the hamlet in broad daylight, ready to kill or to be killed.

The river had different dangers: crocodiles. But of all the animals, the most hated and feared was the huge horse snake. It was sneaky and attacked people and cattle just for the joy of killing. It would either crush its victim to death or poison it with a bite.

Like all farmers' children in the hamlet, I started working at the age of six. My seven sisters helped by working in the kitchen, weeding the garden, gathering eggs, or taking water to the cattle. I looked after the family herd of water buffaloes. Someone always had to be with the herd because no matter how carefully a water buffalo was trained, it always was ready to nibble young rice plants when no one was looking. Sometimes, too, I fished for the family while I guarded the herd, for there were plenty of fish in the flooded rice fields during the rainy season.

I was twelve years old when I made my first trip to the jungle with my father. I learned how to track game, how to recognize useful roots, how to distinguish edible mushrooms from poisonous ones. I learned that if birds, raccoons, squirrels, or monkeys had eaten the fruits of certain trees, then those fruits were not poisonous. Often they were not delicious, but they could calm a man's hunger and thirst.

My father, like most of the villagers, was a farmer and a hunter, depending upon the season. But he also had a college education, so in the evenings he helped to teach other children in our hamlet, for it was too small to afford a professional schoolteacher.

My mother managed the house, but during the harvest season she could be found in the fields, helping my father get the crops home; and as the wife of a hunter, she knew how to dress and nurse a wound and took good care of her husband and his hunting dogs.

I went to the lowlands to study for a while because I wanted to follow my father as a teacher when I grew up. I always planned to return to my hamlet to live the rest of my life there. But war disrupted my dreams. The land I love was lost to me forever.

These stories are my memories. . . .

—H.Q.N.

THE LAND I LOST

TANK, THE WATER BUFFALO

My family had land on which we grew rice. During July to January, the rainy season, the rice field was flooded, and only water buffaloes could be used to till the soil.

We owned three water buffaloes, one male and two females. One day our male died of old age. My father decided to look for the ideal water buffalo to replace him: a bull that was both a hard worker and a good fighter. Fighting ability was important because tigers raided the herd near the edge of the jungle. Buffaloes born and raised among mountain tribes had the reputation of being excellent fighters, but they were often too fierce, violent, and impatient to handle. On the other hand, buffaloes born and raised in the lowlands were patient and obedient, but they did not make good fighters, for they lived in an area where fierce predators did not exist. Neither type of buffalo would meet my father's needs.

However, it was possible to have the ideal buffalo if a young bull had a fierce father from the mountains and a patient mother from the lowlands. This unusual mixture occurred if a fierce mountain bull wandered down to the lowlands and met a female which would bear its offspring. The owner of the female might not know that he had a mixed-blood calf until the calf grew older and the thickness of its coat indicated the mountain origin of its father. So sometimes a farmer who had more buffaloes than he needed would unwittingly sell a valuable mixed-blood calf.

My father, by a combination of luck and patience, discovered a mixed-blood buffalo at the ranch of a buffalo merchant in a town far below the river and bought it at a good price.

I was six years old when my father brought the new calf home. He let me give the young buffalo food and water, and sometimes he allowed me to pat its shoulders. But he told me never to approach it when I was alone, for calves were unpredictable. Although they usually obeyed everybody taller than they were, they did not obey small children and sometimes might hurt them.

I listened to my father, but I trusted our calf. I knew he and I would become great friends.

Our calf grew into a handsome and powerful buffalo. He not only became the head of our small herd, but also became the head of all the herds in our hamlet after many ferocious and successful fights with the other males. We named him "Tank," because when he hit another male during a fight, he struck as heavily as a tank.

One day a young bull from a nearby hamlet trespassed on Tank's territory and challenged his authority. Tank roared a few times to warn the intruder, but the other buffalo was determined to fight. When we heard Tank's roars we knew that there was trouble in the field. Everyone in the hamlet rushed to a hill to watch the fight. We could not prevent it, so we stayed on high ground to protect ourselves; for a defeated buffalo would often run to humans to be rescued and, in its panic, trample them.

Tank left his herd and faced the arrogant intruder. The other buffaloes stopped eating and waited. Suddenly the two bulls charged

3

and ran into each other head on. I heard a mighty thud. Both buffaloes fell back. My heart was pounding. It was the first time any of us had ever seen Tank fall back. Tank was the pride of the hamlet, and we would be very ashamed if he lost the fight; or worse, if Tank were killed, some of our female buffaloes might follow the victorious bull home to the other hamlet, and it would be very hard to bring them back.

The two buffaloes recovered from the powerful collision and ran at each other again. This time they locked horns and tried to twist and break each other's necks. Next, each pushed the other and tried to overturn him. At first the intruder sustained Tank's push very well. But then, little by little, he began to lose ground. Tank pushed him farther and farther backward. Unfortunately for the other buffalo, who had fought quite well so far, there was a deep trench behind him. When his two hind legs fell into the trench, the animal was helpless. Tank's sharpened horns hit first his neck, then his shoulders; but unlike other buffaloes, this one did not call for help.

My father felt sorry for the bull, and he asked my cousin, whom Tank loved the best, to try to stop Tank from killing him. My cousin rushed to Tank's side and called his name. Tank, furious because he was hurt himself, nevertheless listened to my cousin and let him lead him away. The defeated intruder was rescued from the trench and set free, and we never saw or heard from him again.

Tank became so famous that people from far away brought females to breed with him. Buffalo thieves also considered him a prize. One day it rained very hard and Tank did not come home. The next morning we went to look for him. We asked a friend who had a hound dog to help us. My father, my cousin and I, and a few well-armed friends followed the hound and found Tank near a river crossing about fifteen kilometers from home, tied to the root of a tree.

When we untied Tank, he was very happy and licked everybody who had come to rescue him. But we were puzzled. There was blood scattered all around, but Tank himself was unharmed. And why, if thieves had taken Tank so far away from our home, had they finally left him there?

Weeks later these questions were answered. At a local wedding we heard a drunken man tell the story of how he had been hurt by Tank during his attempt to steal him. First, he and two accomplices had spent many days observing the clothes and mannerisms of my cousin, who took care of Tank and his herd. Then, helped by the pouring rain, which prevented Tank from seeing him clearly, and wearing the same clothes and whistling the same song my cousin did, he approached Tank in the field. When he was close enough he seized the rope that passed through the buffalo's nose. Tank was helpless. If he resisted, the rope would hurt his sensitive nose badly. With the help of his two accomplices, the thief led Tank away. When they reached the river crossing, he loosened the rope so Tank could drink some water. But instead of drinking, Tank hit him with his horns, gashing the man's leg from his knee to the upper thigh. Since the man could not walk, the other thieves had to carry him and leave Tank behind. They knew that we would soon be on their trail with a hound dog. But before they left, they managed to tie Tank's rope to the root of a tree so the angered buffalo couldn't attack them again.

When the thief finished his story, one of the wedding guests asked him why he had not killed Tank, since Tank had hurt him so badly. The thief answered that to kill a buffalo, under any circumstances, would bring bad luck. Besides, he admired Tank too much to kill him. He said that if they had succeeded in stealing Tank, they would have been able to sell him for ten times the price of any ordinary buffalo. Then he added that sometimes he still came to our hamlet just to have a look at the magnificent bull. No other bull was intelligent enough to fool him, a man of many years' experience as a buffalo thief. When asked if he would attempt to steal Tank again, he said no, because this time he would be risking his life for sure. He was right. My father had removed the rope passing through Tank's nose, just in case anyone tried to steal Tank again.

To our surprise, we learned we did not need the rope to command Tank. He continued to till the soil and guard the herd. We commanded Tank orally now. He quickly learned the meaning of "Left," "Right," and "Stop," and did exactly what my cousin wanted while working in the field. When my cousin put crops on his back and said, "Go," he would walk straight home by himself. And at home after we had unloaded the crops and said, "Go," he would return to the field.

Other buffaloes might be able to do the same job, but not as well as Tank. Most of them could not resist the green grass that bordered the path leading home. When they lingered to eat, they would be late for their tasks. Or sometimes on their way to the field they would see a female buffalo and would stay around and forget everything. But Tank was so exact about his work that one day an angry housewife said she wished that her husband would be as dependable as Tank.

My cousin also trained Tank to fight jungle cats. He made a stuffed tiger with straw and old linen, and simulated a tiger attack from different angles. He taught Tank to roll over, for without this trick a buffalo was helpless if a tiger or a panther jumped on its back. But a well-trained buffalo could make a tiger jump away by rolling over, or crush it under its weight. And every morning, my cousin attached a razor-sharp knife to each of Tank's horns before he let him go to the pasture on the edge of the jungle.

One afternoon all the buffaloes began roaring. Everyone rushed toward the pasture. Hunters blew their hunting horns, and hunting dogs raced out of houses to follow their masters. When we reached the pasture we saw all the adult buffaloes forming a circle to protect their young, and Tank apart from them, fighting with a huge tiger. As we approached, the tiger quit the fight and limped back into the jungle. We examined Tank and found blood on his horns. There was blood scattered all around the ground too, but it was the tiger that had been badly hurt, not Tank. Tank had only a few scratches on his neck.

After this tangle with the tiger, Tank never had to till the soil again. Other inhabitants of the hamlet told my father that if his two other buffaloes were not enough to till the land he owned, they would send theirs to help. Tank's only responsibility now was to guard the hamlet's herd during the dry season.

MY COUSIN

My cousin stayed with my family from the time that he was a little child because my aunt died during his birth, and my uncle was killed while hunting a wild hog. My parents loved him dearly and tried to give him as much education as they could. They sent him to a good school in the lowlands, but he did not like going to school so far away from the jungle where he was born. My parents finally realized how miserable he was. So my cousin returned home and lived with us.

Even though he was ten years older, my cousin and I were perfect companions, and the best times of my childhood were the times I spent with him. We roamed the jungle behind our hamlet in search of birds' nests, wild hens' eggs, mushrooms, edible fruits; or crossed the

11

river on the backs of water buffaloes to pick green mangoes; or caught fish in the rice fields during the rainy season.

One of my cousin's favorite pastimes was hunting. If the hunt was not to be too dangerous or tiring he would ask my father to allow me to join him. At the end of the rainy season we went hunting wild chickens with a few other boys from the hamlet. Each of us carried a long stick to beat every bush in sight until a frightened chicken was flushed out, and then we chased it, yelling as loud as we could. At this time of the year wild chickens lose their feathers and cannot fly. We just ran after them until they were tired, and we caught them.

When we had enough chickens for the day, we chose a place where we could cook them. We covered their bodies with clay until they looked like soccer balls, and left their legs, necks, and heads free. The bewildered chickens looked comical and pitiful at the same time. We threw them all into the fire until the clay that covered their bodies became white. Then we broke open the white ball of clay and ate the chicken inside. They were delicious!

* * *

One day my cousin climbed a tall banyan tree and brought down a nest of three baby birds. They were all covered with lice. First he got rid of the lice, and then he dug three large holes in the ground and into each hole he put a cage containing a baby bird. He covered the holes with boards, so that each bird would hear only the sounds that he wanted it to imitate. Every day, after feeding them, he let each one hear the same song, again and again. The first bird heard "The Blue Danube Waltz"; the second, "The Bridge over the River Kwai"; and the third, "Maleguena."

After three months, each bird knew its song. My cousin took the cages out of the holes and hung them in three corners of our house. All day long we heard them singing. Sometimes my mother had a headache and would have to ask my cousin to hang the cages in the garden. When guests came to our house they always asked us about the birds. Once in a while we brought the three cages into the sitting room and urged them to sing at the same time. The birds became the celebrities of our hamlet.

One day Tchen, the boy living in the next house, sneaked into our garden and stole the bird that sang "The Blue Danube." He opened the cage door and plucked a few feathers off the bird and scattered them around, to make us think that the bird had been eaten by a cat.

But my cousin noticed that there was no blood around the cage, and instantly suspected Tchen. So when it got dark my cousin posted himself near the window of Tchen's room. He saw Tchen holding the bird in both hands and urging it to sing, but the bird remained silent. My cousin came home looking very pale, and spent the remainder of the night pacing in his room.

Early the next morning, my cousin hid behind a tree on the road that Tchen had to use to go to school. When Tchen walked by, my cousin grabbed him and told him that he'd better return the bird immediately. If he didn't, my cousin would kill him.

Tchen was very frightened, but he still tried to deny he had the bird. My cousin told Tchen what he had seen the night before in his room, and he added that Tchen better not kill the bird to destroy the proof. He meant what he said: the bird back, or death.

Tchen returned the bird. Later on I asked my cousin whether or not he had really meant to kill Tchen. My cousin said: "Yes, I did mean that."

* * *

One day my cousin told me that a man from a tribe nearby had taught him the technique of catching a live python and taming it. Pythons, like wild elephants, can be tamed and become faithful friends to people. My cousin said that when a python attacked you, you should raise both hands high to keep them free while the python coiled around you. Then, with one hand you should grab its tail, and with the other hand you should hold its head away from you, to avoid getting bitten. As the python started squeezing, you should lightly bite its tail. For some reason that would keep the python at bay. Afterward you could call for help if the python was too big, or better yet, walk home with the python wrapped around you. But, my cousin added, you should never make the mistake of biting the python's tail too hard. If you did that, the python would get very angry and squeeze you to death.

A few months later we heard one of our roosters cry very loudly. We rushed out of our house and saw a python squeezing the rooster. My cousin used the technique he had learned and caught the python easily.

We kept the python in a cage, and every day my cousin approached it in a very gentle way. About a week later he succeeded in feeding it a live rat. After that, the python and my cousin quickly became very good friends.

When my cousin was not busy, he applied shoe polish to the python's skin to make it shiny. Sometimes, to entertain a guest at our house, he would make the python into a coil and use it as a pillow. In fact, pythons make very good pillows. Their skins are soft, and their cool blood makes it seem as if your head is resting on an air-conditioned pillow.

I too was very much impressed by my cousin's python and wished I had a smaller one that I could bring with me to the lowlands, where I went to school. It would certainly impress my friends at the boarding house, especially the young daughter of my landlady!

The next time I was home from school, my mother asked my cousin and me to go to the edge of the jungle to gather some firewood. At the jungle's edge we saw birds hopping on the ground and singing in the bushes, a sign that there were no dangerous beasts around. So we went a little farther into the jungle and looked for a type of mushroom my parents were very found of. But secretly, I hoped we might find a small python.

We did not find any mushrooms or pythons, and since we had gathered enough firewood, we started the journey home. A little later we stopped and rested on a fallen tree trunk half buried in dead leaves. My cousin whistled a song and I beat the time to it on the dead tree with my sharp woodcutting knife. Suddenly the tree moved. We looked at each other. Each of us thought that the other had moved the tree. Then we realized that it was not a tree we were sitting on but a very angry python!

We threw everything into the air and ran as fast as we could. When we were far enough away, we looked back and saw the python raising its head about two meters above the ground and opening its huge mouth in our direction. This python certainly wasn't the one I wanted for a pet! And after that whenever we went into the jungle my cousin and I looked very carefully at any tree we wanted to sit on.

THE LONE WILD HOG

The wild hogs living in the jungle near our hamlet were a constant problem because they sometimes attacked people or cattle without provocation. As the guardian of all the buffaloes in our hamlet, Tank once had to fight a huge wild hog when the herd was grazing at the edge of the jungle. He defeated the hog, but the victory was not an easy one.

A fully grown male hog can weigh almost three hundred kilos, and its skin is covered by a thick coating of the sap from a tree we called the "oil tree." A combination of instinct and parasitic itches causes a hog to rub itself up against the oil tree, which oozes sap when its bark is broken. The sap, when condensed and dried, becomes an extremely tough covering

19

that acts like armor, making the wild hogs immune to wounds from short knives or bullets from small guns. The older the hog, the thicker its armor. The only part of the wild hog's body that is not covered by this special sap is its throat and most of its neck, for dry sap would hinder its movement when it wanted to bend its head to drink or to eat roots. That is why the wild hog always rubs away any sap that drops on its neck or its throat.

The head of the wild hog is its most powerful weapon. When a wild hog charges, it may knock down its opponent, but that usually does little damage. It is the follow-up slap of its head that is lethal. The tusks of the wild hog grow in such a way that the sideways slap of its head can rip away the abdomen of a pursuing hunting dog. And even though the tips of an old hog's tusks will tend to curve in toward its head, when an old wild hog is cornered, it will break off the curved parts of its tusks by smashing them against a tree so that the jagged tips will point outward.

Wild hogs live in groups and each group has a leader, or dominant male. Usually, wild hogs try to avoid people, fighting back only when cornered. But every once in a while there will be a lone male that either is not strong

enough to challenge the dominant male of the herd and prefers to live alone, or has been a dominant male of a large group itself, but because of old age has been beaten by an upcoming young male and has had to leave its harem. And it is this lone wild hog that is the most ferocious animal of the jungle. Even a tiger avoids a lone wild hog unless it is very hungry, for it will attack every animal, or person, in sight.

One day a young farmer from our hamlet was working in a cornfield near the edge of the jungle. He had his little daughter and his watchdog with him. His daughter was playing with the dog when suddenly the dog stopped playing and became very nervous. The farmer looked around. He saw a huge wild hog charging down the hill.

There was no place in the field big enough for both the farmer and his daughter to hide, so the farmer picked her up and put her in a small clump of elephant grass. He quickly ran away from the place where he had hidden her, hoping the wild hog would follow him and leave his daughter alone.

As he ran, the farmer yelled as loud as he could for help, while his brave watchdog tried to defend him from the wild hog. The dog was strong, but it was no match for the angry hog. In a few seconds it lay dead on the ground, its chest and its abdomen torn open.

The farmer continued to run toward a tree, but the tree was too far away and the wild hog overtook him. It knocked him to the ground and broke his shoulders and neck with powerful slaps of its head. Four other farmers working in a field nearby rushed over to help their friend, but it was already too late.

The wild hog left the dead farmer and charged the newcomers. They jumped into a deep ditch and tried to hide. By chance, one of them carried with him the horn he used to gather his herd of buffaloes. He blew three blasts on his horn and alerted our hamlet to the danger.

Immediately the whole hamlet was on its feet. Sounds of hunting horns summoning hunting dogs were heard from one end of the hamlet to the other. Meanwhile the man in the ditch kept blowing his horn to let us know exactly where they were.

When the wild hog could not figure out a way to come down into the ditch to attack the men, it stomped around the edge, snorting at them menacingly. As the barks and howls of the hunting dogs became louder and louder, the wild hog gave up and ran back to the jungle. But the dogs saw the wild hog, and the lead dog immediately ran after it.

The village rescue party, including my father and my cousin—whose own father had been killed by a wild hog—pulled the four men out of the ditch. Everyone became very angry when they saw the mangled body of the dead farmer in the field. They found his frightened little daughter hiding in the elephant grass, but they decided not to let the girl see the body of her father. Instead they told her that her father would be okay after a few days of treatment in the hospital, and then someone took the little girl to a neighbor's house.

Judging from the barking of the leader of the hunting dogs, the hog was now far away. It would take a long time for the villagers to catch up with it and then a very long and hard fight to kill it. Nevertheless, even though it was late in the afternoon, they immediately organized the hunt.

First they called in most of their hunting dogs, except for the lead dog and two bloodhounds. The men did not want to tire all the dogs at the same time and thereby maybe lose track of the hog. There was some of the dead farmer's blood on the tusks of the hog, so even if the lead dog were killed, the two bloodhounds would be able to follow the hog's trail.

Next they sent four men to carry the body of their friend home. Then all the rest, armed with knives, quickly moved toward the noise made by the barking lead dog.

The knives they carried were special. Each knife had a long, sturdy handle that ended in a wooden crescent that fit over the hip, and a blade with two sharp edges and a pointed tip, designed to penetrate the hog's throat as far as possible. When a wild hog attacks a hunter he can hold his knife, crescent handle against his hip, and try to stand up to the charge. Or he can sidestep the charge and let the animal come close enough to him to try and slap him with its head. A skillful hunter will let the animal pierce its own throat by slapping it against a well-placed knife.

It was midnight when the men caught up with the hog. They could hear that the dogs had it cornered. It could not run any farther because a steep cliff blocked its way.

The men cut down trees and blocked the only path leading to the hog. Then they let loose ten fresh dogs and called off the lead dog and the two bloodhounds. The fresh dogs harassed the hog for the rest of the night and kept it at bay, tiring it out for the attack at dawn. The men knew they would lose a few dogs, but they had no other choice. If they did not let the dogs attack the hog, it might sneak out of their trap, or even if it did not, fighting a fresh wild hog in the morning would be just as dangerous as fighting a tired hog in the dark.

The night seemed endless. The pandemonium of barking dogs and snorting wild hog kept everyone awake. Once in a while the painful howling of a wounded dog made them sit up with a start and wonder which dog had just been hurt, how many were already dead. The men loved their dogs very much, but they would not hesitate to send in more if the first ten had all been killed. All the rest of the dogs seemed to share the anxiety and the determination of their masters. They lay side by side now without any quarrels; sometimes one licked the nose of another to show that it was friendly. Normally they never got along with each other.

By dawn four dogs were dead, and a fifth was dying. It had a ghastly wound in its stomach, but still it refused to let go of the tail of the angered hog. The other five dogs relentlessly continued to attack.

The hog had a stone wall behind it. Its mouth foamed and its tusks were broken in half. It had prepared itself to fight to the death.

The men let loose all their dogs and then formed two half circles blocking the hog's escape. They let the dogs harass the hog for a while longer and lost a few more dogs; one dog had its two hind legs torn away, but it still tried to crawl forward to bite the hog.

Then, without warning, the hog stopped fighting the dogs and charged the first line of men. The man closest to the hog was lifted off the ground, thrown on his back, and knocked unconscious. The men on either side of him quickly positioned their knives. The hog ignored the unconscious man and slapped its head at one of the other men instead, cutting itself near its ear on his knife. It was a very deep wound, but not a fatal one. The hurt animal ran back to the stone wall, where it was immediately surrounded again by the dogs.

The second line of men quickly replaced the first line, and the unconscious man was carried to safety. He had a broken leg and a bruised hip, but his condition was not critical. Meanwhile the hog, looking very tired now, knelt down and no longer seemed to be bothered by the dogs.

The men called off all the dogs and prepared for the final assault. Two of them slowly approached the hog from either side of its head. The hog got up on its feet again, and moved backward. Then suddenly it charged the man on the right. He jumped aside, but instead of turning, the hog continued its charge and crashed into the first line of men. The two men behind the hog threw away their knives and grabbed its tail and tried to slow it down. The hog quickly turned, but in doing so it slapped into the knife of a man from the first line. It tried to shake off the knife, but the more it tried, the deeper the knife cut into its throat. Finally it succumbed to the fatal wound.

The hunters ignored the dead hog. Instead, some tried to comfort their wounded dogs, while others stared at their dead ones. One of my father's three dogs had had its chest torn open, and died shortly after the fight. His two other dogs stayed next to it and growled at everyone who came close to their dead friend except my father and my cousin.

The men broke into two groups. Some gave first aid to the wounded dogs, while the others cut bamboo trees and vines and built makeshift stretchers to carry the wounded men, the hog, and the wounded and the dead dogs home.

The village chief called a young man to his side and told him to signal on his buffalo horn that the hunting party was safe. The young man blew one long blast followed by one short one and then repeated the signal several times, hoping a favorable wind would carry the happy message home to the hamlet.

When everything was ready, the village chief gave the signal to start the journey home. The blasts on the horn were repeated until the party came in sight of our hamlet. The hunters heard children shouting their names and welcoming them home, and the women ran forward to help the men carry their wounded or dead dogs.

We all gathered at the village chief's home, where the wounded men and dogs were given further treatment and where a big feast of hog meat was prepared. Everyone, including the dogs, had some meat. But the heart of the hog was saved. We placed it on the altar of the young farmer killed in the field. Then we hung the hog's broken tusks in front of his tomb as a reminder to all of us of the constant danger we faced from a lone wild hog.

MISTER SHORT

The river in front of our hamlet was full of crocodiles. These crocodiles were so intelligent that they avoided suspicious live bait or dead poisoned animals, so the villagers abandoned the idea of getting rid of them and we simply learned how to live with them.

Along our stretch of the river lived a crocodile, an old-timer, which the villagers named "Mister Short." Mr. Short—before he became short—used his long tail to knock people out of their boats and then proceeded to eat them.

Our villagers, when going to the town below, always used small boats, and with a small boat one must travel near the riverbank, standing precariously balanced on the moving boat and pushing the boat with a long bamboo stick. It was very easy to be knocked off the boat by one well-placed smack of a crocodile's tail.

Mr. Short had a very simple but ingenious technique for accomplishing this. When a boat passed by his territory, the cunning crocodile stuck his head firmly into the mud of the riverbank and knocked the man off his boat with one powerful lash of his tail. Mr. Short was very successful and had managed to eat quite a few people.

Villagers going downriver through the territory of Mr. Short could avoid the riverbank by poling out to the middle of the river and then letting the current carry the boat. But when they traveled upriver, against the current, they could not avoid poling along the riverbank. It was very difficult to crouch down to avoid the strike of the crocodile and still push the boat against the current with a stick.

One day a young man of our hamlet, Hung, my cousin's friend, was fed up with being terrorized when passing through Mr. Short's territory and decided to do something about it. First he went to the local blacksmith and asked him to forge a very long and sharp knife. During the next few days, with the help of my cousin, Hung spent hours practicing with his new knife. He lay on his back holding his long knife in both hands, and asked my cousin to swing at a gourd hanging over his head with

a long branch of a banana tree. When Hung was skilled enough to cut the banana leaf every time it passed overhead, he next made a dummy of a standing man with a pole in his hands. At sundown Hung and my cousin put the dummy on his boat and traveled to the area where Mr. Short plied his trade.

It was twilight when they got there. Hung lay on his back, facing the standing dummy, and my cousin, holding another knife, hid at the other end of the little boat. They let the boat slide downriver, very close to the riverbank where Mr. Short usually waited in ambush.

In the twilight Mr. Short did not see clearly and mistook the dummy for a real person. The crocodile struck at the dummy with a powerful sideways blow of his tail, and at that very moment Hung swung at the tail with his long knife. He succeeded in cutting off a big portion, which fell into the boat, where it wriggled comically.

After that Mr. Short stopped attacking people, but he lived on for many years, feeding on animals that came to drink at the river. Once in a while people saw him crawling awkwardly into the river, a crocodile with a little tail growing out of the stump of a big tail.

RIVER CREATURES

When my father did not need Tank to till the rice fields during the rainy season, I liked to ride on his back and look for an otters' party. There were many otters living on the riverbanks in front of our hamlet because fish were plentiful in the deep river. Normally the otters lived in twos. But once in a while they all gathered together, caught a great number of fish, and threw them up on the riverbank. Then they all sat down around the fish and ate them. We called this unusual gathering an otters' party.

One day my cousin and I thought up a plan to capture the otters' fish. It would be hard to do because if the otters saw people approaching to try and take their fish, they jumped back into the river and took all the fish with them. But otters did not worry about other animals, so I decided that because Tank's back was wide and high above the ground I could lie flat on his back and approach an otters' party without attracting their attention. To make detection of me even more difficult, I would wear clothes that blended in as much as possible with the color of Tank's back. I would also carry a sturdy stick to scare the otters away in case they turned on me. I had to take this last precaution because I knew that otters, when gathered in a large group, had attacked people who passed by them in small boats.

A few days later I spotted an otters' party on the riverbank. I found a good stick and climbed onto Tank's back. After I showed Tank the direction I wanted him to go, I lay facedown and let him carry me to the party. When Tank was about three meters from the group, I slid down to the ground and chased all the otters into the river. That day I caught them thoroughly by surprise, and I got twenty-four fish, all different kinds, and most of them still intact and fresh.

After that I repeated my raids as often as I could and usually with great success. But one day, after I had surprised the otters and put all the fish on Tank's back, I noticed that one female did not leave. She just swam up and down the river and seemed very anxious to return to where I was. Sensing something unusual, I carefully looked around and discovered three otter cubs in a very deep, narrow hole under a thick thistle bush. I was very excited. Otter cubs were priceless, for one could train an otter cub to catch as many fish as one wanted.

When I had squeezed myself into the hole and had almost reached the cubs, the mother otter came up behind me and bit my toes, very hard! It was so painful that I had to crawl out of the hole as quickly as possible and shake her off. The mother otter jumped back into the river, but when I crawled into the hole again I received the same painful bite on my toes. Suddenly, I came up with an idea. I took some mud from the riverbank and wrote on Tank's back, *Otter cubs—come quickly*. Then I gave Tank a little tap on the back and said, "Go." Tank trotted straight home.

When Tank arrived home my parents saw the fish he carried, but no me. They panicked. Then they discovered the message on Tank's back, and they were very happy. My cousin and Tank soon returned to where I was. My cousin prevented the mother otter from biting me while I took the three cubs out of the hole, one by one.

We sold two of the cubs at the marketplace to two rich merchants, and kept the third one to train to catch fish for us.

The cub we kept quickly learned its job, but we always kept it in an iron cage for fear that it would run away from us. Unfortunately, when I caught the cub its eyes had already opened. If it had just been born and its eyes had not yet opened, we would have been the first beings it saw, and it would have considered us as its parents and remained with us for the rest of its life.

Afterward, whenever we wanted fish we just brought our otter to the riverbank, tied it to a long rope to prevent it from escaping, and let it dive into the river. When it caught a fish, it surfaced and gave the fish to us.

Since it was always easy for us to get fish, we gave them to friends whenever they wanted any. Sometimes, when we had free days, we let our otter fish all day long. It caught a great number of fish, which we then dried and sent to our relatives who weren't as lucky as we to have a trained otter for a fisherman.

*　*　*

In the river in front of our hamlet there lived a type of catfish that weighed more than one hundred kilos when fully grown. Gourmets sought them, but they were difficult to catch because they often broke the fishline or tore up the fishnet. We called them white catfish in order to distinguish them from black catfish, which were darker and smaller.

To catch white catfish we used a squirrel or a big frog as bait. We couldn't use fishing poles made of light bamboo trees because they would break. And big, heavy poles were too tiring to hold. Thus a fisherman who wanted to catch a white catfish just held the fishline firmly in his hands. When the catfish bit, the fisherman held the line for a while. If the line did not break and the catfish tired, he slowly pulled it to the riverbank and used a big net to pull it onto dry ground.

One day I left Tank and the other buffaloes grazing near the river while I talked with a friend of my family's. He was old and could not do hard work in the field, so he fished for white catfish to help out his family. I had just finished saying that if a fish took the bait, I would help him, when I saw his face turn pink and his hands shake very hard. Immediately I jumped next to him, grabbed the line, and started pulling.

The fish fought back like a devil, and one of its powerful jerks almost dragged both of us into the river. I yelled to Tank to come and help us.

Tank came quickly. We tied the fishline to his horns and signaled him to walk backward. Tank lowered his head and pulled with all his strength. Luckily, the line held, and Tank dragged the fish closer and closer to shore. Suddenly we saw a huge white catfish jump into the air and then fall back into the water with a tremendous splash. Tank kept pulling and the old man kept yelling, "That's right, son. That's right, son." Moments later we saw the head of the fish come out of the water, then the body, and finally the tail.

When the entire fish was on the riverbank, we stopped Tank and untied the line from his horns. Our old friend was so happy that he jumped up and down like a child. He said that without me and Tank he knew that the catfish would have gotten away from him. Then we brought Tank closer to the fish so that he could see it clearly. Tank looked at the fish and pricked up his ears in a funny way.

My old friend called it a day, because he had made a big catch and he wanted to go home immediately to show his family. But the fish was too heavy for him to carry. Although it was still early, I decided to bring the herd home so that Tank could help our friend carry the fish.

I told our friend that we should load the fish on Tank's back. He was very happy with the idea, but said that first he had to cut off the fish's pectoral fins. He explained to me that each pectoral fin has a spine with venom in it that made a cut from the fin very painful. He took a knife out of his pocket, cut off the two pectoral fins, and thereby prevented Tank from being hurt.

When we arrived at my house, where I left the herd, the old friend wanted to give my parents part of the fish. But my parents refused his offer, telling him that our otter caught all the fish we needed. They said he should keep the whole fish and sell it at the marketplace, where he would get a good price for such a delicacy.

Tank and I accompanied our friend to his house. When we arrived, his family was very happy to see the big fish. The old man kept repeating how wildly the fish had fought and how helpful Tank and I had been.

Soon all his children got busy. Several carried the fish inside, one prepared tea for him, and another hung his fishing line on the wall. When the boys and girls were tired of looking at the fish, they surrounded Tank and asked me endless questions about him: Why was Tank's stomach so big? Was he pregnant? Why were the hairs at the end of his tail longer than those on his head? And so on.

My friend's wife wanted me to stay for dinner, but I refused because my parents had told me to be back as soon as possible. My mother wanted to use Tank to draw some water from the well. But as I said good-bye, my friend's wife made sure I didn't refuse a piece of cake to eat on the way home, and a lump of brown sugar for Tank. Tank was very fond of brown sugar—more than he was of fishing, I think!

* * *

From the time Tank helped our old friend to get the white catfish, I had considered the idea of catching golden eels with Tank's help. There were two kinds of golden eels living in our area—one kind had bulging eyes, the other had beady eyes. Both were very much sought after because their meat was excellent. These eels, when matured, reached two meters in length and weighed about five kilos.

The eels lived in muddy ditches that brought water to the fruit gardens, the banana groves, and the coconut groves when the level of the water in the river in front of our hamlet was high. They hid in deep holes that they dug in the hard clay soil beneath the mud of the ditch, usually near a tree planted on the border of the ditch. The roots of the tree were a natural barrier against intruders, and when an eel coiled its body around the root of a tree, it was almost impossible to pull it out. Each eel's nest had several openings to allow it to escape in case of danger, and inside a nest there were many zigzag corners, which allowed an eel to hook its body around a corner and resist someone's trying to pull it out by its head or tail.

Eels lay constantly in ambush near the main entrance of their nest, waiting for prey to pass by—fish, shrimp, crabs, even baby ducks if a mother duck was foolish enough to lead her young brood over an eel's nest. Then the eel would shoot out of its nest like an arrow, snap up a baby duck, pull it down into its nest, and swallow it moments later. Sometimes an eel even tried to attack an adult duck if food was scarce. It would bite the duck's foot and try to pull the frightened fowl down into the nest, where it would drown. The duck might survive if someone heard it quack and rushed to rescue it, but it would often lose one foot because the teeth of a golden eel are very sharp.

One could lure an eel with almost any kind of bait, but we used earthworms because they were easy to find. We would dangle the worm at the nest's entrance, and sooner or later the eel would come out and bite the bait. We allowed the eel to swallow the bait far down into its stomach, instead of pulling the line right away, for if we pulled the line too soon we would only succeed in tearing off the eel's jaw during the struggle to pull it out of its nest. But with a hook in its stomach, it could not get away—no matter how hard it tried. Sooner or later, unless the fishing line broke, we would drag the eel out of its nest, dead or alive.

In our hamlet, whenever an eel was hooked, the children of the neighborhood had

a good time. They ran out of their houses when they heard the yell for help. Two or three boys would help pull out the eel, and everyone else yelled or laughed. Sometimes adults came to help too, if they were not busy. It took at least one hour to pull the eel out of its nest, and by this time, it was usually dead.

But a live eel got a better price than a dead one in the market, and since Tank had easily succeeded in pulling the white catfish out of the river for our old friend, I came up with the idea of letting him drag eels out of their nests for me. If he could pull an eel out quickly, I had a better chance to get the eel alive instead of dead.

First I had to find an eel's nest, but this was not difficult. One can know roughly the location of a nest by listening carefully to the sound an eel makes when it snaps at a victim. The sound made by its closing jaws is similar to that of a loud click and can be heard clearly from thirty or forty meters away, especially at night.

After finding the general area of a nest, I pinpointed the exact location by examining the mud. The mud around the main entrance of the nest is always more disturbed than the rest.

Then I tied the end of a fishing line to Tank's horns and made the bait jump up and down on the mud covering the hole. The eel stuck its head out of the mud first, saw the bait clearly, snapped it up, and returned to its nest below. I loosened the line to let the eel swallow the bait into its stomach, then I signaled Tank to pull. Despite his tremendous strength, Tank needed quite a bit of effort to pull the eel out of its nest. But it was the most exciting sight to see the wagging head of the eel stick out of the mud first, and then its big, trembling golden body come slowly out of the hole. When the eel was on dry ground, it yanked, turned, and squirmed like an earthworm attacked by a swarm of fire ants.

Using this method, I caught several big eels; none of them could resist Tank more than fifty counts. When Tank started pulling, I counted, One, two, three . . . Some strong eels reached forty-five, but the weaker ones were already on dry ground, wriggling, when I had not yet reached twenty. Often, when an eel had taken the bait, I yelled to my friends to come to see Tank's work. When everybody arrived, I signaled Tank to pull. Some of my friends counted with me while the others yelled, clapped their hands, or cheered loudly for Tank.

It was difficult to tell whether Tank enjoyed fishing for eels as much as we did, but he always accomplished his task extremely well.

THE HORSE SNAKE

Despite all his courage there was one creature
in the jungle that Tank always tried to avoid—
the snake. And there was one kind of snake
that was more dangerous than other snakes—
the horse snake. In some areas people called
it the bamboo snake because it was as long as
a full-grown bamboo tree. In other regions, the
people called it the thunder or lightning snake,
because it attacked so fast and with such power
that its victim had neither time to escape nor
strength to fight it. In our area, we called it
the horse snake because it could move as fast
as a thoroughbred.

One night a frightened friend of our family's banged on our door and asked us to let
him in. When crossing the rice field in front

of our house on his way home from a wedding, he had heard the unmistakable hiss of a horse snake. We became very worried; not only for us and our friend, but also for the cattle and other animals we raised.

It was too far into the night to rouse all our neighbors and go to search for the snake. But my father told my cousin to blow three times on his buffalo horn, the signal that a dangerous wild beast was loose in the hamlet. A few seconds later we heard three long quivering sounds of a horn at the far end of the hamlet answering our warning. We presumed that the whole hamlet was now on guard.

I stayed up that night, listening to all the sounds outside, while my father and my cousin sharpened their hunting knives. Shortly after midnight we were startled by the frightened neighing of a horse in the rice field. Then the night was still, except for a few sad calls of nocturnal birds and the occasional roaring of tigers in the jungle.

The next day early in the morning all the able-bodied men of the hamlet gathered in front of our house and divided into groups of four to go and look for the snake. My father and my cousin grabbed their lunch and joined a searching party.

They found the old horse that had neighed the night before in the rice field. The snake had squeezed it to death. Its chest was smashed, and all its ribs broken. But the snake had disappeared.

Everybody agreed that it was the work of one of the giant horse snakes which had terrorized our area as far back as anyone could remember. The horse snake usually eats small game, such as turkeys, monkeys, chickens, and ducks, but for unknown reasons sometimes it will attack people and cattle. A fully grown horse snake can reach the size of a king python. But, unlike pythons, horse snakes have an extremely poisonous bite. Because of their bone-breaking squeeze and fatal bite they are one of the most dangerous creatures of the uplands.

The men searched all day, but at nightfall they gave up and went home. My father and my cousin looked very tired when they returned. My grandmother told them to go right to bed after their dinner and that she would wake them up if she or my mother heard any unusual sounds.

The men went to bed and the women prepared to stay up all night. My mother sewed torn clothing and my grandmother read a novel she had just borrowed from a friend. And for

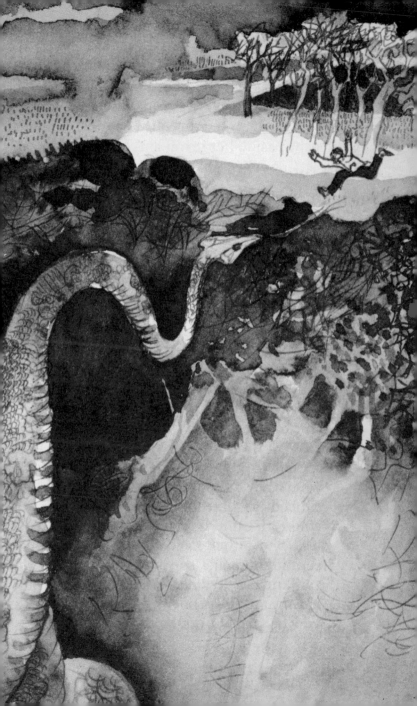

the second night in a row, they allowed my little sister and me to stay awake and listen with them for as long as we could. But hours later, seeing the worry on our faces, my grandmother put aside her novel and told us a story:

Once upon a time a happy family lived in a small village on the shore of the South China Sea. They respected the laws of the land and loved their neighbors very much. The father and his oldest son were woodcutters. The father was quite old, but he still could carry home a heavy load of wood.

One day on his way home from the jungle he was happier than usual. He and his son had discovered a wild chicken nest containing twelve eggs. Now he would have something special to give to his grandchildren when they pulled his shirtsleeves and danced around him to greet him when he came home.

The father looked at the broad shoulders of his son and his steady gait under a very heavy load of wood. He smiled. His son was a good son, and he had no doubt that when he became even older still his son would take good care of him and his wife.

As he was thinking this he saw his son suddenly throw the load of wood at a charging horse snake that had come out of nowhere. The heavy load of wood crashed into the snake's head and stunned it. That gave them enough time to draw their sharp woodcutting knives. But instead of attacking the horse snake from the front, the elder shouted to his son to run behind the big bush of elephant grass nearby while he, who was a little too old to run fast, jumped into the front end of the bush. Each time the snake passed by him the old man managed to hit it with his knife. He struck the snake many times. Finally it became weak and slowed down; so he came out of his hiding place and attacked the snake's tail, while his son attacked the snake's head. The snake fought back furiously, but finally it succumbed to the well-coordinated attack of father and son.

When the snake was dead, they grabbed its tail and proudly dragged it to the edge of their village. Everyone rushed out to see their prize. They all argued over who would have the honor of carrying the snake to their house for them.

The old woodcutter and his son had to tell the story of how they had killed the snake at least ten times, but the people never tired of hearing it, again and again. They all agreed that the old woodcutter and his son were not only brave but clever as well. Then and there the villagers decided that when their chief, also a brave and clever man, died, the old woodcutter was the only one who deserved the honor of replacing him.

When my grandmother finished the story, my little sister and I became a bit more cheerful. People could defeat this dangerous snake after all. The silent darkness outside became less threatening. Nevertheless, we were still too scared to sleep in our room, so my mother made a makeshift bed in the sitting room, close to her and our grandmother.

When we woke up the next morning, life in the hamlet had almost returned to normal. The snake had not struck again that night, and the farmers, in groups of three or four, slowly filtered back to their fields. Then, late in the afternoon, hysterical cries for help were heard in the direction of the western part of the hamlet. My cousin and my father grabbed their knives and rushed off to help.

It was Minh, a farmer, who was crying for help. Minh, like most farmers in the area, stored the fish he had caught in the rice field at the end of the rainy season in a small pond. That day Minh's wife had wanted a good fish for dinner. When Minh approached his fish pond he heard what sounded like someone trying to steal his fish by using a bucket to empty water from the pond. Minh was very angry and rushed over to catch the thief, but when he reached the pond, what he saw so petrified him that he fell over backward, speechless. When he regained control he crawled away as fast as he could and yelled loudly for help.

The thief he saw was not a person but a huge horse snake, perhaps the same one that had squeezed the old horse to death two nights before. The snake had hooked its head to the branch of one tree and its tail to another and was splashing the water out of the pond by swinging its body back and forth, like a hammock. Thus, when the shallow pond became dry, it planned to swallow all the fish.

All the villagers rushed to the scene to help Minh, and our village chief quickly organized an attack. He ordered all the men to surround the pond. Then two strong young men approached the snake, one at its tail and the other at its head. As they crept closer and closer, the snake assumed a striking position, its head about one meter above the pond, and its tail swaying from side to side. It was ready to strike in either direction. As the two young men moved in closer, the snake watched them. Each man tried to draw the attention of the snake, while a third man crept stealthily to its side. Suddenly he struck the snake with his long knife. The surprised snake shot out of the pond like an arrow and knocked the young man unconscious as it rushed by. It broke through the circle of men and went into an open rice field. But it received two more wounds on its way out.

The village chief ordered all the women and children to form a long line between the open rice field and the jungle and to yell as loudly as they could, hoping to scare the snake so that it would not flee into the jungle. It would be far easier for the men to fight the wounded snake in an open field than to follow it there.

But now there was a new difficulty. The snake started heading toward the river. Normally a horse snake could beat any man in a race, but since this one was badly wounded, our chief was able to cut off its escape by sending half his men running to the river. Blocked off from the river and jungle, the snake decided to stay and fight.

The hunting party surrounded the snake again, and this time four of the best men attacked the snake from four different directions. The snake fought bravely, but it perished. During the struggle one of the men received a dislocated shoulder, two had bruised ribs, and three were momentarily blinded by dirt thrown by the snake. Luckily all of them succeeded in avoiding the fatal bite of the snake.

We rejoiced that the danger was over. But we knew it would only be a matter of time until we would once again have to face our most dangerous natural enemy—the horse snake.

OPERA, KARATE, AND BANDITS

When she was eighty years old my grandmother was still quite strong. She could use her own teeth to eat corn on the cob or to chew on sugar plants to extract juice from them. Every two days she walked for more than an hour to reach the marketplace, carrying a heavy load of food with her, and then spent another hour walking back home. And even though she was quite old, traces of her beauty still lingered on: Her hands, her feet, her face revealed that she had been an attractive young woman. Nor did time do much damage to the youthful spirit of my grandmother.

One of her great passions was theater, and this passion never diminished with age. No matter how busy she was, she never missed a show when there was a group of actors in town. If no actors visited our hamlet for several months, she would organize her own show in which she was the manager, the producer, and the young leading lady, all at the same time.

My grandmother's own plays were always melodramas inspired by books she had read and by what she had seen on the stage. She always chose her favorite grandson to play the role of the hero, who would, without fail, marry the heroine at the end and live happily ever after. And when my sisters would tell her that she was getting too old to play the role of the young heroine anymore, my grandmother merely replied: "Anybody can play this role if she's young at heart."

When I was a little boy my grandmother often took me to see the opera. She knew Chinese mythology by heart, and the opera was often a dramatization of this mythology. On one special occasion, during the Lunar New Year celebrations—my favorite holiday, because children could do anything they wanted and by tradition no one could scold them—I accompanied my grandmother to the opera.

When we reached the theater I wanted to go in immediately. But my grandmother wanted to linger at the entrance and talk to her friends. She chatted for more than an hour. Finally we entered the theater, and at that moment the "Faithful One" was onstage, singing sadly. The "Faithful One" is a common character in Chinese opera. He could be a good minister, or a valiant general, or someone who loved and served his king faithfully. But in the end he is unjustly persecuted by the king, whose opinion of him has been changed by the lies of the "Flatterer," another standard character.

When my grandmother saw the "Faithful One" onstage she looked upset and gave a great sigh. I was too interested in what was happening to ask her the reason, and we spent the next five hours watching the rest of the opera. Sometimes I cried because my grandmother cried at the pitiful situation of the "Faithful One." Sometimes I became as angry as my grandmother did at the wickedness of the "Flatterer."

When we went home that night my grandmother was quite sad. She told my mother that she would have bad luck in the following year because when we entered the theater, the "Faithful One" was onstage. I was puzzled.

I told my grandmother that she was confused. It would be a good year for us because we saw the good guy first. But my mother said, "No, son. The 'Faithful One' always is in trouble and it takes him many years to vindicate himself. Our next year is going to be like one of his bad years."

So, according to my mother's and grandmother's logic, we would have been much better off in the new year if we had been lucky enough to see the villain first!

* * *

My grandmother had married a man whom she loved with all her heart, but who was totally different from her. My grandfather was very shy, never laughed loudly, and always spoke very softly. And physically he was not as strong as my grandmother. But he excused his lack of physical strength by saying that he was a "scholar."

About three months after their marriage, my grandparents were in a restaurant and a rascal began to insult my grandfather because he looked weak and had a pretty wife. At first he just made insulting remarks, such as, "Hey! Wet chicken! This is no place for a weakling!"

My grandfather wanted to leave the restaurant even though he and my grandmother had not yet finished their meal. But my grandmother pulled his shirt sleeve and signaled him to remain seated. She continued to eat and looked as if nothing had happened.

Tired of yelling insults without any result, the rascal got up from his table, moved over to my grandparents' table, and grabbed my grandfather's chopsticks. My grandmother immediately wrested the chopsticks from him and struck the rascal on his cheekbone with her elbow. The blow was so quick and powerful that he lost his balance and fell on the floor. Instead of finishing him off, as any street fighter would do, my grandmother let the rascal recover from the blow. But as soon as he got up again, he kicked over the table between him and my grandmother, making food and drink fly all over the place. Before he could do anything else, my grandmother kicked him on the chin. The kick was so swift that my grandfather didn't even see it. He only heard a heavy thud, and then saw the rascal tumble backward and collapse on the ground.

All the onlookers were surprised and delighted, especially the owner of the restaurant. Apparently the rascal, one of the best karate fighters of our area, came to his restaurant every day and left without paying for his food or drink, but the owner was too afraid to confront him.

While the rascal's friends tried to revive him, everyone else surrounded my grandmother and asked her who had taught her karate. She said, "Who else? My husband!"

After the fight at the restaurant people assumed that my grandfather knew karate very well but refused to use it for fear of killing someone. In reality, my grandmother had received special training in karate from my great-great uncle from the time she was eight years old.

Anyway, after that incident, my grandfather never had to worry again. Anytime he had some business downtown, people treated him very well. And whenever anyone happened to bump into him on the street, they bowed to my grandfather in a very respectful way.

* * *

When my father was about ten years old a group of bandits attacked our house. There had been a very poor harvest that year, and bandits had already attacked several homes in other hamlets. My grandmother had a premonition this would also happen to them, so she devised a plan. In case of danger, she would carry the children to safety, and my grandfather would carry the bow and arrows, a bottle of poison, and the box containing the family jewels.

It was night when the bandits came. My grandfather became scared to death and forgot his part of the plan, but my grandmother remained very calm. She led her husband and children to safety through a secret back door that opened into a double hedge of cactus that allowed a person to walk inside, undetected, to the banana grove. When they were safely inside the banana grove, my grandfather realized that he had forgotten the bow and arrows and the bottle of poison. So my grandmother stole back into the house and retrieved the weapons.

The bandits were still trying to smash through our very solid front door when she sneaked out of the house for the second time. She dipped one arrow in poison and crawled around to the front of the house near the bandits. But, upon second thought, she put the poisoned arrow aside and took another arrow and carefully aimed at the leg of the bandit leader. When the arrow hit his thigh the bandit let out a loud cry and fell backward.

The night was so dark that none of the

bandits knew where the arrow had come from. And moments later, friends started arriving and began to attack them from the road in front of our house. The bandits panicked and left in a hurry. But my grandmother spent the rest of the night with her family in the banana grove, just in case the bandits came back.

* * *

When my grandmother became older she felt sick once in a while. Before the arrival of the doctor, she would order everybody in the house to look sad. And during the consultation with the doctor she acted as if she were much sicker than she really was. My grandmother felt that she had to make herself look really sick so that the doctor would give her good medicine. She told the doctor that she had a pain in the head, in the shoulders, in the chest, in the back, in the limbs—pain everywhere. Finally the doctor would become confused and wouldn't know what could be wrong with her.

Whenever the doctor left, my mother would sneak out of the house, meet him at the other side of the garden, and tell him exactly where my grandmother hurt.

Two or three days later my grandmother usually felt much better. But before the doctor arrived for another visit she ordered us to look

sad again—not as sad as the first time, but quite sad. She would tell the doctor that her situation had improved a little bit but that she still felt quite sick. My grandmother thought that if she told the doctor she had been feeling much better he would stop giving her good medicine. When the doctor left my mother sneaked out of the house again and informed him of the real condition of my grandmother.

I don't think my grandmother ever guessed it was my mother's reports to the doctor, and not her acting, that helped her get well.

* * *

One morning my grandmother wanted me to go outside with her. We climbed a little hill that looked over the whole area, and when we got to the top she looked at the rice field below, the mountain on the horizon, and especially at the river. As a young girl she had often brought her herd of water buffaloes to the river to drink while she swam with the other children of the village. Then we visited the graveyard where her husband and some of her children were buried. She touched her husband's tombstone and said, "Dear, I will join you soon." And then we walked back to the garden and she gazed at the fruit trees her husband had planted, a new one for each time she had given birth to a child. Finally, before we left the garden my sister joined us, and the two of them fed a few ducks swimming in the pond.

That evening my grandmother did not eat much of her dinner. After dinner she combed her hair and put on her best dress. We thought that she was going to go out again, but instead she went to her bedroom and told us that she didn't want to be disturbed.

The family dog seemed to sense something was amiss, for he kept looking anxiously at everybody and whined from time to time. At midnight my mother went to my grandmother's room and found that she had died, with her eyes shut, as if she were sleeping normally.

It took me a long time to get used to the reality that my grandmother had passed away. Wherever I was, in the house, in the garden, out on the fields, her face always appeared so clearly to me. And even now, many years later, I still have the feeling that my last conversation with her has happened only a few days before.

SO CLOSE

My grandmother was very fond of cookies made of banana, egg, and coconut, so my mother and I always stopped at Mrs. Hong's house to buy these cookies for her on our way back from the marketplace. My mother also liked to see Mrs. Hong because they had been very good friends since grade-school days. While my mother talked with her friend, I talked with Mrs. Hong's daughter, Lan. Most of the time Lan asked me about my older sister, who was married to a teacher and lived in a nearby town. Lan, too, was going to get married—to a young man living next door, Trung.

Trung and Lan had been inseparable playmates until the day tradition did not allow them to be alone together anymore. Besides, I think they felt a little shy with each other after realizing that they were man and woman.

Lan was a lively, pretty girl who attracted the attention of all the young men of our hamlet. Trung was a skillful fisherman who successfully plied his trade on the river in front of their houses. Whenever Lan's mother found a big fish on the kitchen windowsill she would smile to herself. Finally she decided that Trung was a fine young man and would make a good husband for her daughter.

Trung's mother did not like the idea of her son giving good fish away, but she liked the cookies Lan brought her from time to time. Besides, the girl was very helpful; whenever she was not busy at her house Lan would come over in the evening and help Trung's mother repair her son's fishing net.

Trung was happiest when Lan was helping his mother. They did not talk to each other, but they could look at each other when his mother was busy with her work. Each time Lan went home Trung looked at the chair Lan had just left and secretly wished that nobody would move it.

One day when Trung's mother heard her son call Lan's name in his sleep, she decided it was time to speak to the girl's mother about marriage. Lan's mother agreed they should be married and even waived the custom whereby the bridegroom had to give the bride's family a fat hog, six chickens, six ducks, three bottles of wine, and thirty kilos of fine rice, for the two families had known each other for a long time and were good neighbors.

The two widowed mothers quickly set the dates for the engagement announcement and for the wedding ceremony. Since their decision was immediately made known to relatives and friends, Trung and Lan could now see each other often.

One day as Trung helped Lan to plant a mango tree behind her house, he asked her: "Have you ever looked at those dainty town boys who pass by your house all the time?" Instead of answering Trung, Lan poked a hard finger at his ribs and laughed. Then she said: "You are not bad looking at all; so don't bother about them. Besides, my mother said that in darkness everything, everybody looks the same!" To a shy young man like Trung the remark was quite bold, but he was very pleased and happy.

At last it was the day of their wedding. Friends and relatives arrived early in the morn-

71

ing to help them celebrate. They brought gifts of ducks, chickens, baskets filled with fruits, rice wine, and colorful fabrics. Even though the two houses were next to each other, the two mothers observed all the proper wedding day traditions.

First Trung and his friends and relatives came to Lan's house. Lan and he prayed at her ancestors' altars and asked for their blessing. Then they joined everyone for a luncheon.

After lunch there was a farewell ceremony for the bride. Lan stepped out of her house and joined the greeting party that was to accompany her to Trung's home. Tradition called for her to cry and to express her sorrow at leaving her parents behind and forever becoming the daughter of her husband's family. In some villages the bride was even supposed to cling so tightly to her mother that it would take several friends to pull her away from her home. But instead of crying, Lan smiled. She asked herself, why should she cry? The two houses were separated by only a garden; she could run home and see her mother anytime she wanted to. So Lan willingly followed Trung and prayed at his ancestors' altars before joining everyone in the big welcome dinner at Trung's house that ended the day's celebrations.

Later in the evening of the wedding night Lan went to the river to take a bath. Because crocodiles infested the river, people of our hamlet who lived along the riverbank chopped down trees and put them in the river to form barriers and protect places where they washed their clothes, did their dishes, or took a bath. This evening, a wily crocodile had avoided the barrier by crawling up the riverbank and sneaked up behind Lan. The crocodile grabbed her and went back to the river by the same route that it had come.

Trung became worried when Lan did not return. He went to the place where she was supposed to bathe, only to find that her clothes were there but she had disappeared. Panic-stricken, he yelled for his relatives. They all rushed to the riverbank with lighted torches. In the flickering light they found traces of water and crocodile claw prints on the wet soil. Now they knew that a crocodile had grabbed the young bride and dragged her into the river.

Since no one could do anything for the girl, all of Trung's relatives returned to the house, urging the bridegroom to do the same. But the young man refused to leave the place; he just stood there, crying and staring at the clothes of his bride.

Suddenly the wind brought him the sound of Lan calling his name. He was very frightened, for according to an old belief a crocodile's victim must lure a new victim to his master; if not, the first victim's soul must stay with the beast forever.

Trung rushed back to the house and woke all his relatives. Nobody doubted he thought he had heard her call, but they all believed that he was the victim of a hallucination. Everyone pleaded with him and tried to convince him that nobody could survive when snapped up by a crocodile and dragged into the river to be drowned and eaten by the animal.

The young man brushed aside all their arguments and rushed back to the river. Once again, he heard the voice of his bride in the wind, calling his name. Again he rushed back and woke his relatives. Again they tried to persuade him that it was a hallucination, although some of the old folks suggested that maybe the ghost of the young girl was having to dance and sing to placate the angry crocodile because she failed to bring it a new victim.

No one could persuade Trung to stay inside. His friends wanted to go back to the river with him, but he said no. He resented them for not believing him that there were desperate cries in the wind.

Trung stood in front of the deep river alone in the darkness. He listened to the sound of the wind and clutched the clothes Lan had left behind. The wind became stronger and stronger and often changed direction as the night progressed, but he did not hear any more calls. Still he had no doubt that the voice he had heard earlier was absolutely real. Then at dawn, when the wind died down, he again heard, very clearly, Lan call him for help.

Her voice came from an island about six hundred meters away. Trung wept and prayed: "You were a good girl when you were still alive, now be a good soul. Please protect me so that I can find a way to kill the beast in order to free you from its spell and avenge your tragic death." Suddenly, while wiping away his tears, he saw a little tree moving on the island. The tree was jumping up and down. He squinted to see better. The tree had two hands that were waving at him. And it was calling his name.

Trung became hysterical and yelled for help. He woke all his relatives and they all rushed to his side again. At first they thought that Trung had become stark mad. They tried

to lead him back to his house, but he fiercely resisted their attempt. He talked to them incoherently and pointed his finger at the strange tree on the island. Finally his relatives saw the waving tree. They quickly put a small boat into the river and Trung got into the boat along with two other men. They paddled to the island and discovered that the moving tree was, in fact, Lan. She had covered herself with leaves because she had no clothes on.

At first nobody knew what had really happened because Lan clung to Trung and cried and cried. Finally, when Lan could talk they pieced together her story.

Lan had fainted when the crocodile snapped her up. Had she not fainted, the crocodile surely would have drowned her before carrying her off to the island. Lan did not know how many times the crocodile had tossed her in the air and smashed her against the ground, but at one point, while being tossed in the air and falling back onto the crocodile's jaw, she regained consciousness. The crocodile smashed her against the ground a few more times, but Lan played dead. Luckily the crocodile became thirsty and returned to the river to drink. At that moment Lan got up and ran to a nearby tree and climbed up it. The tree was very small.

Lan stayed very still for fear that the snorting, angry crocodile, roaming around trying to catch her again, would find her and shake her out of the tree. Lan stayed in this frozen position for a long time until the crocodile gave up searching for her and went back to the river. Then she started calling Trung to come rescue her.

Lan's body was covered with bruises, for crocodiles soften up big prey before swallowing it. They will smash it against the ground or against a tree, or keep tossing it into the air. But fortunately Lan had no broken bones or serious cuts. It was possible that this crocodile was very old and had lost most of its teeth. Nevertheless, the older the crocodile, the more intelligent it usually was. That was how it knew to avoid the log barrier in the river and to snap up the girl from behind.

Trung carried his exhausted bride into the boat and paddled home. Lan slept for hours and hours. At times she would sit up with a start and cry out for help, but within three days she was almost completely recovered.

Lan's mother and Trung's mother decided to celebrate their children's wedding a second time, because Lan had come back from the dead. All their friends came and sang to the happy couple. At midnight, at the end of the last serenade, "The Wedding Night," the bride and bridegroom were supposed to open the windows of their room to thank the minstrels. But Lan and Trung kept the window closed. Perhaps they were too tired or too busy to open it. The serenade party left good-humoredly, saying one could do well only one thing at a time!

LITTLE ALTAR ON
THE ROADSIDE

When I went to the rice field with Tank, my mother often wanted me to burn some incense at a little altar along the roadside. Sometimes I lingered there for a while and cut off the vines that crawled over the altar. But I never lingered if it was growing dark, for at night the deserted road leading to the field seemed too sad and lonely because of the presence of the little altar.

In a little house near the southern end of our hamlet lived a widow and her young son. With the help of her relatives and friends she had brought up her son since the death of her husband, who was killed by a lone wild hog. This woman was still very young at the time of her husband's death, but she refused to remarry, despite many proposals from other men, because she dearly loved her husband. The image of his mangled body remained as vivid in her mind as if the accident had happened yesterday.

When her son was old enough she told him of her wish to see him married. She told him that she became lonely when he was working in the field, that her eyes were not good enough anymore to sew his torn clothes, that he needed a wife to help him at home, and that she needed grandchildren to make her life less lonely. She also told him that since he was the only male left in his family, if something happened to him there would be nobody to continue his father's line and no one to take care of the tombs of his ancestors.

Her son listened to his mother. He agreed that the greatest disgrace for the dead was for nobody to take care of their graves, or burn incense in front of their tombs after having cleared the weeds away during the Lunar New Year. So a few weeks later a go-between found him a bride in a nearby village.

Three days before the wedding the son went to the jungle to cut down some bamboo trees to make a new bed for himself and his bride. He built the bed but he did not use it, because according to tradition the wedding bed had to remain as virginal as the bride and the bridegroom. So for three nights he slept on a bench on the veranda of his house.

The night before the wedding his mother could not sleep because of a strange sense of foreboding. She got up and walked to the side of her sleeping son. In the semidarkness, she could not see his face clearly at first. When she looked closer she saw a large banyan leaf entirely covering his face. She jumped back and leaned on the door and tried to recover from the shock of this dreadful sight. She was upset because people always covered the face of the dead with a banyan leaf. When she felt calm enough she tiptoed to her son's side, gently took the leaf away, and then stayed near him for a while before going back to her room.

But once again the mother could not fall back to sleep. So in a little while she got up and came to see her son. For the second time she saw her son's face covered with a banyan leaf. This time she decided to find out who had done this most unlucky thing.

She removed the leaf and pretended to go back to her room, but when she had passed the half-opened door she turned back and hid behind it. A few minutes later she saw a mouse

dragging a large banyan leaf and covering her son's face with it. Struck by terror at this omen, she fell down and lost consciousness.

When she came to, the night was still young, so she decided to spend the rest of it at her son's side. She decided not to tell him what she had seen, because if she did she would spoil his wedding. But after the wedding she would persuade her son to give up his profession as a woodcutter and convince him to become a carpenter or a blacksmith. Then he would have nothing to do with the hazardous jungle or the unpredictable river.

Early in the morning of the day of the wedding, she went to visit her husband's grave and prayed to him to protect their only son. Next she went to the village chief and told the chief what she had seen the night before. She asked the chief to forbid her son to perform any dangerous duties during the next few months. Then she went home and prepared the food and drink for the wedding.

Everyone in our hamlet came to the wedding and brought gifts, except the minstrel. He did not bring anything because his gift was to entertain the others with his songs. The rest of the day the mother was distracted by the laughter and cheerful conversation of the guests and by the minstrel's songs instructing the bride and the bridegroom in their new responsibilities as husband and wife. She was even happy with the appearance of the bride, whom she saw for the first time that day. The young girl was not pretty, but she looked very healthy. There was no doubt in the mother's mind that she would soon have grandchildren and that they would brighten her house in the days ahead.

However, her son seemed not to be in touch with what was going on. He laughed and forced himself to smile at his friends' silly remarks about the wedding night, but his smiles always turned into strange grimaces at the end.

In the evening when the last guest had gone, the mother went to her room. She was exhausted. Suddenly at midnight the hysterical cries of the bride woke her. She ran to their room and found her son convulsing uncontrollably, saliva coming out of his mouth. Her son tried to hold on to his mother's hands. In a barely audible voice he whispered, "Mother, help me. Mother, help me."

She quickly pushed the bride out of the room and told her to yell as loudly as she could to alarm the neighborhood. By the time the closest neighbor arrived the son had let go of his mother's hands and his bewildered eyes had become empty. And while the first arrival looked on, the mother closed her son's eyes, touched his face, and then dropped dead at his side.

The death of the bridegroom apparently had been caused by poison, since his skin grew pink and there was no insect bite or injury of any sort on his body. The bride was charged with murder, and according to the laws of the land she would be hanged if she could not prove her innocence. All during the funeral the bride clung to the coffin of her husband and kept begging him to wake up and tell people that she had not killed him.

The coroner felt sorry for the young bride and made a special effort to look into the matter. First he went to the hamlet where her parents lived and made a thorough inquiry about her life before her marriage. He learned that she had had no lover and that her parents had been glad she was getting married because they still had many more daughters who needed husbands. After his inquiry he did not find any reason why the girl should have killed her husband.

Returning home, the coroner made one last effort to save the girl by examining the wedding bed. He spotted a little hole in the bamboo near the head of the bed. He held his breath and examined the hole closely. Suddenly he jumped back. His vision was blurred by some invisible vapor coming out of the little hole.

With the consent of the village chief he broke the bamboo bed, and out jumped a small two-steps snake. It tried to get away, but the villagers chased after it and killed it. The snake must have been in the bamboo tree since hatching. Its mother, in her wandering life, had laid an egg in the hole created by some insect while the tree was still young. The taller the tree grew the narrower the hole became, and when the baby snake hatched it was trapped in the tree forever. It must have stayed alive by depending upon the rain and dew and the stray ants or insects that accidently fell into the hole. Since it didn't use its venom often it had built up a lot of poison, and the breath of the snake would be strong enough to kill a person who breathed it. So the bridegroom, sleeping with his nose near the hole, had been killed by the snake's breath, and not by his wife.

The bride sold the little house and returned to her parents. At first she came back every once in a while to visit the graves of her husband and his family and to clear the weeds which grew on them. But then she did not come anymore. She remarried and lived with her new husband far away from our hamlet. So the people of our hamlet built a little altar on the side of the road leading to the graves of the son and mother and father, and during the holidays someone always burned incense at their altar, and from time to time travelers stopped by and prayed at the roadside altar, hoping their prayer would make their long journey less hazardous.

But most importantly, the lonely little altar on the roadside reminded us that just down the deserted road there were three tombs to take care of, especially during the Lunar New Year.

THE HERO

Horse snakes, despite their strength and venom, have one soft spot. They are very fond of the burning oil made of the fat of the hogfish. We call it that because this fish, when fully grown, can get as big and fat as a wellfed hog. However, to catch a hogfish you need to do it in a special way.

When a hogfish takes the bait it always fights very hard, and most of the time it succeeds in getting off the hook. But a wise fisherman will very slowly coax a hogfish to the surface and then gently scratch its belly. After having been sufficiently scratched, the fish will let four or five men take it wherever they wish.

The flesh of the hogfish is very good to eat. But its fat is even more precious because the smell of the oil made from this fat will, when burned, intoxicate a horse snake. So at night, whenever we went from one place to another in our hamlet, we used lamps filled with hogfish oil to ward off any sudden attacks by horse snakes. If we crossed the path of a horse snake, the smoke of the lamps would make it tipsy. The snake might follow the lamp for a while in order to inhale more smoke, but it would totally forget about attacking us.

During the six-month rainy season, most of the river fish swim into the shallow water of the rice field and live there, feeding on all kinds of insects. Then during the dry season they return to the river. In addition most of the tropical fish in the area also have the ability to live out of the water for more than two hours, staying on paths and dikes where they can find more insects at night.

My cousin and I liked to go out into the field and catch fish at night. Whenever we went out we always carried a hogfish oil lamp. Since I could not catch fish as well as my cousin, who was ten years older, I carried the lamp and a bucket to put the fish in, and my cousin carried a long knife to kill any fish that we found near the edge of the water. But he preferred to catch them alive.

One evening when we were in the field, my cousin began teasing me, saying that since I carried the hogfish oil lamp, a horse snake would follow us home. I knew that he was teasing, but I was frightened and looked back every so often to make sure that there was no horse snake following us. Then suddenly I saw a huge horse snake, coming from nowhere, and following me with its head waving unsteadily. I was so terrified that I couldn't speak; I could barely drag my feet. Luckily my cousin stopped and tried to catch a fish lying in the middle of the path. I bumped into him and almost knocked him over. Surprised at my unusual clumsiness, he looked back and saw the horse snake behind me. He was terrified too, but instinctively he swung his knife and struck the snake in the head. We dropped everything and ran home as fast as we could, more frightened than ever by the great noise the snake made behind us.

When we reached home my father gathered all his friends to search for the snake. He felt that since it had been discovered so nearby they ought to try to destroy it as soon as possible.

When we returned to the place where my cousin and I had encountered the snake, we

saw, to our great surprise and relief, that the snake was lying there dead. With extraordinary luck, my cousin had hit the snake right in the middle of its head and split its brain.

The snake was so heavy that it took eight men to carry it home. The next day it was on display in front of our house. Everybody was impressed by its size. To fight against a snake of this length twenty men usually were needed.

My cousin put some coconut oil on his hair to make it shinier and he stayed around near the snake. The young girls smiled at him a little bit more than usual, and the young men seemed jealous.

My cousin was a hero!

THE MONKEY AND THE
OLD LADY

During the harvest season, Tank and I often hid behind a thick bush and waited for monkeys to come to steal the crops. When they sneaked into the field, I would give the signal to Tank to charge the monkey thieves. Tank would roar really loud while I yelled and shot at them with my slingshot. We tried to scare them away, but they always came back a few days later. Sometimes they knew where we were hiding and made faces at us from a distance or did somersaults on the plants to taunt us.

The river that crosses the rice field in front of our hamlet was a lifeline, not only for the people of our hamlet, but also for all the animals from the nearby jungle and mountains. Man and beast came to the river daily. But unlike the other wild animals, which came to the river only at night in order to avoid humans, monkeys came to it any time they wanted to, often after having just stolen some food from the field.

These monkeys were so intelligent that the farmers could not get rid of them. They avoided the most ingenious traps, and there were not enough guns to shoot them down from a distance. So we had to learn how to live with them and to make the best use of them we could.

A fully grown male monkey can weigh fifty kilos. With its intelligence and agility it can be a good fighter, but it usually has no heart for fighting. However, although it can be the most cowardly of all the animals in the jungle, it can also be the most malicious! A small boy with a stick can chase a whole herd of wild monkeys, if he acts brave and looks fierce. But if he doesn't look fierce, the monkeys will turn on him and kill him.

Nevertheless, most of the people in our hamlet kept a monkey or two in their houses for certain purposes, such as picking coconuts or hunting squirrels, or just as pets. But they were kept in strong cages or chained to sturdy poles or trees.

One day an old lady who was a friend of our family's showed my mother a baby monkey that had been born in captivity. Because the old lady had no children or other relatives left, she dearly loved her baby monkey. Each day she carried the monkey around in one hand, like a newborn child, and in the other hand she carried a bottle of milk.

Things went well for six months, and then the monkey began to behave mischievously. My mother suggested the monkey be chained to a tree, because if it tried to run away, the old lady was too slow to catch it. When the old lady hesitated, my mother said: "My good friend, you should not only chain your monkey to a tree but also inspect the chain every day. You came to live in our hamlet only a short while ago and you may not know how mischievous, malicious, and unpredictable these monkeys can be.

"Quite a few years back when I was still a young girl there was a butcher living with his wife and his two-year-old daughter at the edge of our hamlet. The butcher had a monkey chained to a pole above his pigsty. He had the strange idea that its tricks might entertain the hogs below and make them grow faster. Each day he went about his job cutting up meat, under the watchful eyes of the monkey.

"One evening his neighbor next door invited him and his wife to dinner. Because they were afraid their two-year-old daughter might disturb their hosts, they left her sleeping quietly in the cradle. Since the two houses were separated only by a thin bamboo wall, they could get back immediately to their house if the child woke up and wanted them.

"During the dinner the monkey managed to get loose from its chain. It grabbed the same knife that the butcher used to kill hogs and ran into the house and slaughtered the child, cutting it into pieces exactly as the butcher did the hogs. The child did not cry or make any noise, so perhaps the monkey killed it when it was sound asleep.

"When the couple got home the sight of their dismembered child horrified them. Their cries of distress gathered many friends who began a thorough search of the area for the monkey, but the monkey had already disappeared into the jungle, a few hundred meters away.

"The butcher was never the same again. For many years afterward he constantly looked for his monkey, but he never found it. Sometimes people saw him, haggard, roaming the jungle.''

Reluctantly, the old lady listened to my mother's story, but she seemed to love and trust the little monkey as much as the day it was born. She continued to take good care of it, and she was so proud when it learned how to shake hands with her.

When the monkey was two years old it was much bigger and stronger than most monkeys in the area because the old lady had fed it well. People saw her talking to the monkey for hours as if it understood everything she said. Sometimes she woke up in the middle of the night and missed her monkey so much that she lit a candle and went out to see if it was all right.

Every three days she went to the marketplace to buy food for herself and bananas for her monkey. Since matches were very scarce at the time, whenever she left home for such a journey, she buried the burning embers in the hearth under a thick layer of ashes in order to keep the fire going.

One morning she buried the burning embers, said good-bye to her monkey, and left for the marketplace as usual. But that day the monkey managed to get free from its chain after

she had left, and the first thing it did was to dig out the burning embers and put them on the thatched roof of the house. The house burned down completely. Meanwhile, the monkey seemed to know what it had done to the old lady, because it disappeared immediately.

When the old lady returned, both her monkey and her house were gone. She cried so hard, not only from sadness but also from anger. My parents invited her to stay with us until we could raise enough money to build her a new house.

After that day she always carried a stick with her, intending to beat the monkey any time she could lay a hand on the unfaithful beast. My mother thought that she would be too slow to catch the monkey, but she did not try to discourage her from attempting to punish him.

One day the old lady came home very excited. "I saw him! It was him! With a bunch of other wild ones. He made fun of me by jumping up and down. I wanted to teach him a lesson but he ran away quickly. The next time he will not be so lucky as this time!"

Soon afterward a friend of hers recognized her monkey among the wild ones and killed it with a poisoned arrow. He thought that it would please his old friend very much. But when he showed her dead monkey to her she wasn't happy. Instead she stared at the dead body and cried and cried for hours.

WHAT CAN YOU DO
WITH A MONKEY?

Our family had a small coconut grove near the edge of the jungle and my father trained a monkey to pick coconuts for him. But it took my father quite a while to train our monkey for the job.

One day a peddler from the lowlands stopped by our house to show my father his goods. Since my father was very proud of our monkey, he showed it to the peddler. When the peddler heard that my father had taken several months to train our monkey he told us that he wouldn't need that much time to train not only one, but even a bunch of monkeys to do different useful tasks. My father was very interested in what the peddler said and invited him to stay with us overnight so that he could show us how to train a monkey quickly.

Early the next morning the peddler, my father and a few of his friends, my cousin, and I went to the riverbank near a big tree that had branches hanging above the water. We hid ourselves carefully and waited for the monkeys to come to the river for their morning drink.

Monkeys never come right down to the river because of the mud. Instead they use a special technique to reach the water. The first monkey hangs on to a branch over the water with one hand while the other hand holds the hand of the second monkey. The second monkey holds the hand of a third monkey and so on until one of the hanging chain of monkeys is close enough to the water to drink. The rest of the monkeys drink by changing positions in the chain.

That morning the level of the water in the river was quite low. Fifteen monkeys were needed to form a complete chain. A friend of my father's shot the topmost monkey, and the rest of the chain fell into the river. Since monkeys cannot swim well we caught all fourteen, tied their hands behind their backs, and marched them home like prisoners of war.

When we reached home the peddler chose

one monkey that looked very mean and seemed to be the leader of the group. Then he lined up the others in front of the mean-looking one. Next he tried to teach the mean-looking monkey how to use a spoon to eat rice. He repeated the process about ten times, but the sullen monkey refused to learn. So the peddler asked for a knife and cut off the head of the stubborn monkey in front of the others.

The other monkeys trembled and remained extremely quiet. Then when the peddler handed each of them a spoon and a bowl of rice they all used the spoons and ate the rice properly.

During the rest of the day the peddler quickly taught them to draw water from the well with a bucket, pick up trash and carry it to the dump, and so on. Sometimes the monkeys were slow to learn something new or became unruly; but when the peddler showed them the knife, they all became orderly and the learning proceeded in a proper way.

The next day a friend of my family's who liked tea very much asked if he could have one of the captured monkeys to use to pick tea leaves in the mountains for him. Because of the cooler temperatures, tea grown on mountaintops is much better than tea grown at the foot of the mountains. My father said yes.

Our friend began training the monkey by feeding it a mixture of water and opium residue every evening. After one week the monkey became addicted. Then he took it into the mountains.

At first our friend had to climb to the top of the mountain each day with the monkey to show it how to tell tea leaves apart from other leaves by smelling them, and then how to pick the leaves and put them into a light basket attached to its back. In the meantime, the monkey kept drinking the opiated water every night when it got back to its master's home.

After a week the monkey knew its job exactly. Our friend set it free in the morning, and in the evening it brought home a basketful of tea leaves. Some days the monkey did not pick enough tea leaves, and on those days our friend did not allow it to drink the special water. The next day the monkey would do a better job.

Since our friend could not drink all the tea his monkey picked, he sold some of it. He made quite a bit of money by doing so. If someone criticized him he would say: "It is better to be an addicted monkey than a chicken beheaded and eaten!"

My father decided to teach one of the newly captured monkeys how to hunt squirrels. Anyone who owns coconut groves knows that squirrels are the most destructive animals. Of course some young coconuts were always lost to giant bats and rats, but when the coconuts that escaped damage became ripe and were ready for market, the squirrels would come. They would eat through the coconut shells with their sharp teeth, drink the milk, eat the coconut meat, and then relax inside the shells, which made very comfortable nests.

Squirrel hunting required a very well trained monkey, a dog, and hunters with slingshots. Hunters shot at squirrels with their slingshots. They were happy if they could hit one and slow it down, but their main purpose was to tire out the squirrel by constantly harassing it until it would hide on the top of a coconut tree. Then the hunters would send the monkey up the tree to catch the tired squirrel and throw it down to the dog below. The owners of the coconut groves gave the hunters some money for each squirrel and then hung the dead squir-

rels on the coconut trees, hoping to scare away other squirrels.

In order to train his new monkey how to hunt squirrels, my father organized a special hunt and brought the new monkey along with him. My father waved a knife in front of it and the new monkey quickly learned to catch squirrels and throw them to the dog. The monkey seemed a little bit bewildered when it went up the tree to get the first squirrel, but by the time it caught its third squirrel it seemed to enjoy the work. It held the frightened squirrel by the tail, swinging it to and fro and making faces at it before throwing it to the waiting dog. Everybody agreed that the monkey had become a full-fledged hunter in record time.

THE "UNFAITHFUL BIRDS"

Often, when I was in the fields and the sun was high in the sky, I would stay in the shade of a tall banyan tree and listen to the song of a bird we called the "unfaithful bird." And just as often, when I woke up in the middle of the night and listened to the sounds of the jungle, the confused noises of the deep forest would be interrupted by a few clear, lonely notes from the song of an unfaithful bird. Usually, their song was lively and made me forget everything. But sometimes they would sing a melancholy song. Then I longed for something other than the world I lived in. Maybe it was just their night song that stirred this longing in me, for some people say unfaithful birds are not really awake at night; they say they are just singing their dreams. . . .

We called them unfaithful birds because they never stayed with people, no matter how hard you tried to keep them. But first you had to catch them! They built their nests on trees where wasps and killer bees lived, making the task of reaching their nests nearly impossible. Nevertheless, some villagers managed to catch baby birds, even before they had opened their eyes, hoping that when they did—four days after they were hatched—the birds would consider the humans their parents and stay with them. But that never really worked. As soon as the birds learned to fly they would flee immediately.

When I was seven years old, my cousin gave my younger sister and me a nest of six young unfaithful birds. He avoided the wasps and killer bees by stealing the nest at night. My father built us an attractive cage, and my sister and I spent hours every day catching grasshoppers, crickets, and other insects to feed to the ever-hungry baby birds.

One day I told my cousin that we were very tired of catching insects. I asked him whether he knew a better way to keep the birds. My cousin said yes, there was a way; the birds had to be addicted to opium. He told me that the merchant living on the other side of our garden smoked opium and that I should ask him for the sticky residue inside his opium pipe. If I could get the merchant to give me the residue, my cousin would show me how to use it to make the birds stay with us.

As a matter of fact, the merchant was a friend of mine. From time to time my mother allowed my sister and me to cross the garden and peer through the hedge to watch him smoke opium in his small room. He always smoked at six in the evening, with all the windows open. Sometimes my sister and I arrived a bit early and watched how he prepared for his smoking session. We tried to hide from him, but he usually saw us. Instead of being angry, he simply smiled vaguely.

He owned a black dog and had four white lizards that lived on the ceiling of his room. The dog and lizards looked restless and unhappy until he started smoking. Then the opium smoke hung around the room and the animals became relaxed and happy. The dog slowly wagged his tail and got a dreamy look in his half-shut eyes, which were as dreamy as those of his master. The lizards made chuckling noises and little taps on the ceiling with their little tails.

So the next day when my sister and I saw the merchant sitting in front of his house, we went over to him immediately. I brought along my mandolin even though I hardly knew how to play it. But I played my best to accompany my sister, and she sang as loudly as she could. When we finished the song the merchant smiled at us and said, "Young lady and young gentleman, it was very nice of you to sing a song for me. Now what can I do for you?" I said, "Sir, we have six unfaithful birds and my sister and I have had a hard time catching insects to feed them. As you know, they will fly away if I set them free and let them feed themselves. But my cousin told us that if you gave us the residue that sticks in your opium pipe, he knows a way for us to keep the birds without feeding them."

The merchant gave us what we wanted, adding that if we needed more we should simply let him know. When we returned home my cousin mixed the residue in a liter of water. Then each day at six P.M. he let the birds drink the water from this bottle. Within six days, the birds would become restless around six o'clock and wait anxiously for their opium drink. But after having drunk the water they looked very happy and preened themselves or sang nicely. My cousin told us that now it was time to set them free.

The next morning we opened the door of the cage; all six birds quickly escaped and flew straight ahead without looking back at us. Even though we knew beforehand this would probably happen, my sister and I were still upset. We remembered all those weeks we had worked very hard to take care of them. But around six o'clock, just as my cousin had predicted, one by one they flew back to the cage and waited restlessly for their special drink. When we gave it to them they drank it greedily, and then looked very contented with themselves. Some sang, some preened themselves. At one point four or five of them sang at the same time, and produced a very beautiful symphony.

This situation lasted for many months, and the birds became the talk of our small hamlet. Neighbors would drop in around six o'clock and watch the birds return for their drink and then listen to their singing.

But one day a very strong storm hit our hamlet around six o'clock. When it was over our birds did not come back. My sister and I waited for them all evening until finally our parents made us go to bed. The next day we

found our birds, one by one, a few steps from each other, lying dead on the ground. They were killed because the storm had hit just when they were flying back to their cage. Maybe they were weak after months of having their special drink, or maybe they needed the special drink so much that they couldn't wait until the storm was over to fly back.

We looked at them for a long time and cried. We buried them in six little tombs, side by side, in a corner of our garden.

THE TWO-STEPS
SNAKE

When there wasn't much work to do in the fields, my cousin and I often went into the woods, looking for birds' eggs. We always brought Tank with us because then I could sit high on Tank's back and inspect the tops of bushes while my cousin could explore the areas underneath on foot. We were almost always successful and brought home all kinds of eggs: wild duck eggs, wild chicken eggs, songbird eggs, and once, an egg we had never seen before.

On that day, my cousin and I found an egg a little too big for any kind of songbird and a little too small for a chicken or duck. We decided to bring it home and ask my parents what it was. After examining it my father guessed that it could be a snake's egg. My mother wanted us to throw it away immediately, but my father said we could keep it in a little glass case, for he was quite curious about it himself.

A few days later to our great excitement, a two-steps snake broke out of the shell. My mother was scared and insisted that we keep the baby snake in its case somewhere in our garden, for two-steps snakes belonged to the most poisonous species of snakes in our region.

It got its name from the fact that if it bites someone, he will walk only two more steps, then fall dead. A fully grown snake will measure about one meter. In general it is not aggressive. But it's dangerous because it also never runs away from anything, especially when it sheds its skin and hides either underwater in the rice field or under dead leaves in the forest to protect its tender new skin. A person may go out at that time of the year to catch fish in the rice field or to gather firewood in the forest and, by accident, step on a newly molted snake. And in self-defense, it will bite.

The two-steps snake does not live in the same place for very long, unlike most other snakes. Instead it wanders around to look for frogs or mice, and when its hunger is satisfied it finds a new hiding place and stays there for a while. Therefore, during the mating season the female may scatter her eggs over quite a large area. In most cases these eggs are hatched by the heat of the sun. But a bird on a nest may wake up to see a small snake come out of one of the eggs it considers its own, or a housewife may find a few eggs under her pile of firewood, or a woodcutter may be surprised when a small snake jumps out of a hole in a piece of wood he has just chopped. Of course, many of the scattered eggs will be swallowed by other snakes, or eaten by monkeys, wildcats, birds, or other animals. Only eggs that are well hidden survive.

Our two-steps snake grew quite fast. Every day either my cousin or I went to the far end of our garden, where we had placed the glass case, and fed the snake. Each time we threw in a live fly or small grasshopper, the insect was killed instantly by the breath of the snake, which had poisoned the air in the case.

A few weeks passed and our snake started to become restless. One day when we approached the case to feed the snake, it angrily opened its mouth and we saw its sharp fangs. We were frightened because the glass was fragile, and there would be little chance for us to get away from the quick-moving snake if it broke the case.

When we told my parents what had happened they made us get rid of the snake at once. We covered the case with piles of straw and burned it. When the snake was dead, my father took it out of the case and burned it again, thoroughly. Afterward he threw its ashes into the river. He said that if we threw the snake away without burning it, one day someone might step on its jaw and be killed. The poison in the fangs always remained, and many people had been killed by stepping on dead two-steps snakes.

Months later we found another two-steps snake under the bamboo bush in front of our house. The bamboo bush was intertwined with other bushes that surrounded the house, so we could not easily uproot it in order to kill the snake. Besides, it would have been useless work if the hole in which the snake lived reached under other bushes too. We just hoped that the snake would go away in a week or so, for according to an old belief, if one set out to kill a two-steps snake and failed, it would sneak into the house at night and kill all of the family. We did not believe in this legend, but since we could not find a sure way to kill the snake, we did not like to tempt the fates.

However, unlike other two-steps snakes, this one seemed to choose the shelter beneath the bamboo bush as its semipermanent nest. It did go away, once in a while, for a week or ten days, but it always came back. Little by little we accepted its presence and gave up the idea of killing it.

The snake seemed not to be bothered by us either. Occasionally we saw it sunbathing or receiving a friend. Its friend was a bit longer, but we did not know whether it was a male or a female. Sometimes in the moonlight the two snakes danced together. First, each one made a coil and faced the other. Then they raised their heads at the same time and swayed backward and forward. After a while the heads would move up and down, or sometimes they stayed still with their mouths nearly touching. After each visit our snake would accompany its friend to the gate of our house.

We had a watchdog who was very fascinated by the snake, and vice versa. When the snake disappeared, the dog seemed to miss it. The dog looked into its hole or walked around the bamboo bush, making a whining sound. But when the snake was around, the two always kept a certain distance between themselves; the

dog could kill the snake by snapping its neck, and the snake could kill the dog by biting him. When the snake was sunbathing, the dog came as close as he dared and watched the snake with a funny look in his eyes. Sometimes he wagged his tail, pricked up his ears, and barked at the snake in a friendly way. The sunbathing snake kept its eyes half shut in a dreamy way. But in reality it watched every move of the dog warily.

One morning we found the dog dead in the courtyard. At first we thought that the snake had bitten him, but we couldn't find any bite on the dog's body. When we opend the dog's stomach we found a poisoned piece of meat. We suspected that a thief had poisoned our dog in order to get into our house.

That evening we asked a few friends to stay overnight for a couple evenings to help us watch for the thief. On the next two nights nothing happened. But at two o'clock in the morning on the third night my cousin, who was on watch, heard a loud shriek followed by a heavy thud. He woke up everybody, and we all grabbed weapons, but decided not to go out into the dark. The rest of the night was still except for a few calls of night birds and the occasional roar of tigers in the jungle.

Early in the morning we found the dead body of a man near the two-steps snake's nest. We carefully examined the body of the stranger and found a snake bite on his ankle. Quickly the news spread that the snake had avenged the death of its friend, the dog, by killing the thief who had poisoned him.

Within a few days the snake had become our "guardian," one who would punish anyone who tried to hurt us. The news spread so fast that soon travelers came from afar to visit the place where the snake lived. Parents would bring their newborn children to see the snake so that the children would grow up free from evil. When farmers came, they would bring a chicken or a duck and set it loose near the snake as a sacrifice to the "guardian."

In a short time there were so many chickens and ducks that we didn't know what to do with them. Ducks filled the ponds, and there were chickens in the rice field, chickens in the garden, chickens in the bamboo bushes. Sometimes a hen disappeared for about three weeks and suddenly reappeared with a very noisy brood of chicks. The chickens and ducks made so much noise in the morning that it was quite impossible to sleep past dawn.

I was going away to school in the lowlands

by then, and from time to time I asked a friend: "Would you like to have a chicken?" When he or she said yes, the next Monday I brought a very big chicken from home for my friend. After a while everyone began calling me "Chicken Boy."

The snake worshippers kept coming and the number of chickens and ducks kept increasing. There was no way to convince other people that the snake was not a "guardian genius." Once, during the endless years of fighting in Vietnam, a rocket blew up the bamboo bush. But the snake escaped without any injury and its prestige increased in the eyes of its worshippers.

As time passed the snake trusted us more. From time to time my nephew threw it a live frog or a mouse. Sometimes it came as close as half a meter from my nephew to pick up a crippled frog and to swallow it on the spot.

The last time I heard from my mother, the snake was still alive but quite old. Perhaps because of its old age, its snake friend had stopped coming to visit. In its loneliness it seemed to be more attracted to our new watchdog, which was as friendly to the snake as our first one had been.

SORROW

Winter nights on the central highlands of Vietnam are very cold. Sometimes when the wind was howling outside and we were huddling around the fireplace, I worried about Tank and the rest of the herd. But my father told me that water buffaloes adapt themselves very well to the cold weather, because they are much bigger and stronger than we are. And sure enough in the morning when I touched their shoulders, I found they were quite warm. And when I gave them food and water they drank and ate heartily.

One day when I was in the field with the herd, fierce fighting between the French forces and the Resistance led by Ho Chi Minh erupted in our hamlet. The battle was so close that I

tried to run away and find shelter in the river nearby.

I led Tank and the rest of the herd toward the river, but suddenly I noticed that Tank was lagging behind and limping. I ran back and saw that Tank had been hit by a stray bullet which had passed through his chest. With my urging, Tank made it to the river, but he looked very weak when he lay down. I tapped Tank's neck slightly to let him know that I was still with him, and I also tried to tell him that he would be okay. I saw tears in Tank's eyes, but I did not know whether he suffered from the bullet wound or whether he was sad because he was going to die. When the battle was over, Tank could not get up. He died about an hour later.

We buried Tank in the graveyard where we buried all the dead of our family, and every Lunar New Year my father burned incense in front of all the tombs, including Tank's.

About the Author

HUYNH QUANG NHUONG was born in Mytho, Vietnam. Upon being graduated from Saigon University with a degree in chemistry, he was drafted into the South Vietnamese army. Mr. Huynh was permanently paralyzed by a gunshot wound received on the battlefield, and in 1969 he came to the United States for additional medical treatment.

Since then Mr. Huynh has earned bachelor's and master's degrees in French and comparative literature from Long Island University and the University of Missouri and now makes his home in Columbia, Missouri. THE LAND I LOST is his first book.

About the Artist

VO-DINH MAI was born in Hue, Vietnam. He studied at the Lycée of Hue, and at the Sorbonne, the Académie de la Grande Chaumière, and the Ecole Nationale Supérieure des Beaux-Arts in Paris.

Mr. Vo-Dinh is a professional artist whose works have been exhibited in thirty-six one-man shows both here and abroad and have appeared on UNICEF greeting cards. He has illustrated a score of books, including his own THE TOAD IS THE EMPEROR'S UNCLE and the Christopher Award-winning book written by his wife, Helen Coutant, FIRST SNOW.

He and his wife have two daughters, Phuong-Nam and Linh-Giang, and currently live in Burkittsville, Maryland.